GW00503786

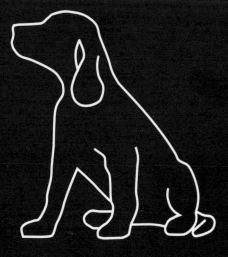

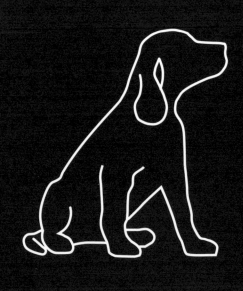

Photographs by Araldo De Luca

Editorial Project : Valeria Manferto De Fabianis ~ Graphic Design : Clara Zanotti ~ Text : Giorgio Ferrero

L FOR **LABRADOR**

WHITE STAR PUBLISHERS

If dogs run free,
then what must be,
must be, and that is all.
True love can make a blade
of grass / Stand up straight and tall.
In harmony with the cosmic sea / True
love needs no company / It can cure the
soul, it can make it whole / If dogs run
free. **(Bob Dylan, If Dogs Run Free)**
So, of one thing I am sure / It's a
friendship so pure / Angels singing
all around my door so fine.
Yeah, ain't but one thing
to do / Spend my natural
life with you, / You're the
finest dog I knew so fine.
(Led Zeppelin,
Bron-Y-Aur Stomp)

Rêveur Sognatore Träumer Soñador

Dreamer

Back...

Verso...   Retro...   Hinten...   Detrás ...

... Front

Lazy

Paresseux
Svogliato
Lustlos
Desganado

Fugitive

Fugitif   Latitante   Selbstvergessen   Fugitivo

Bored

Aburrido

Gelangweilt

Annoiato

Ennuyé

16

Wakening

Réveil

Risveglio

Aufwachen

El despertar

19

Guilty !

Coupable! Colpevole! Schuldig! Culpable!

Embarassed

Embarrassé Imbarazzato Verlegen Avergonzado

Ready to go !

Prêt à partir !
Pronti via !
Bereit zum Aufbruch !
Listo para ir !

Diabolic

Diabolique Diabolico Teuflisch Diabólico

Possessive

Possessif   Possessivo   Besitzergreifend   Posesivo

Mocking

Narquois Beffardo Spöttisch Burlón

Somnolent Assonnato

Sleepy

Müde Soñoliento

Wise

Sage   Saggio   Weise   Sabio

Inquisitive

Intrigué   Incuriosito   Neugierig   Intrigado

Sad

Triste   Triste   Traurig   Triste

Actor

Acteur   Attore   Schauspieler   Actor

Gluttonous

Gourmand Goloso Leckermaul Glotón

Brave

Courageux   Coraggioso   Mutig   Valiente

Singing context

Agile

Agile   Agile   Flink   Ágil

Greco-Roman Wrestling

Lutte gréco-romaine
Lotta greco-romana
Griechisch-römischer Ringkampf
Lucha griego-romana

Unconditional surrender

Capitulation sans condition

Resa incondizionata

Bedingungslose Kapitulation

Rendición

Dialogue

Dialogue   Dialogo   Zwiegespräch   Diálogo

Tussle

Confusion   Confusione   Verwirrt   Confusión

In white...

En blanc... In bianco... Weiß... En blanco...

... et noir   ... e nero   ... und schwarz   ... y negro

... and black

Playful

Joueur

Giocoso

Verspielt

Jocoso

Irresistible
temptations

Irrésistibles tentations

Irresistibili tentazioni

Unwiderstehlich

Tentaciónes irresistibles

Playtime

Récréation   Ricreazione   Zeit zum Spielen   Recreo

Upside-down vision

Vision invertida

Von unten betrachtet

Visione ribaltata

Vision renversée

Méditation   Meditazione Meditation   Meditación

Meditation

Aristocratic

Aristocratique   Aristocratico   Aristokrat   Aristocrático

Pedigree

Lignée   Discendenza   Abstammung   Descendencia

Gentleman

Gentilhomme Gentiluomo Kavalier Caballero

Impatient

Impatient   Insofferente   Ungeduldig   Intolerante

Holiday

Vacances
In vacanza
Ferien
Vacación

Worn-out

Épuisé   Esausto   Erschöpft   Agotado

Expectation

Attente

Attesa

Erwartungsvoll

Espera

Gun dog

Chien d'arrêt

Cane da riporto

Apportierhund

Perdiguero

Close encounters

Rencontres du troisième type

Incontri ravvicinati

Unheimliche Begegnung

Encuentros cercanos

In love

Amoureux   Innamorato   Verliebt   Enamorado

Hautain Altezzoso Hochmut Altanero

Haughty

Predator

Prédateur
Predatore
Räuber
Depredador

Languid

Langoureux   Languido   Schmachtend   Lánguido

In disgrace !

En punition !   In castigo !   In Ungnade gefallen !   Castigo !

Bothered

Contrarié
Contrariato
Besorgt
Contrariado

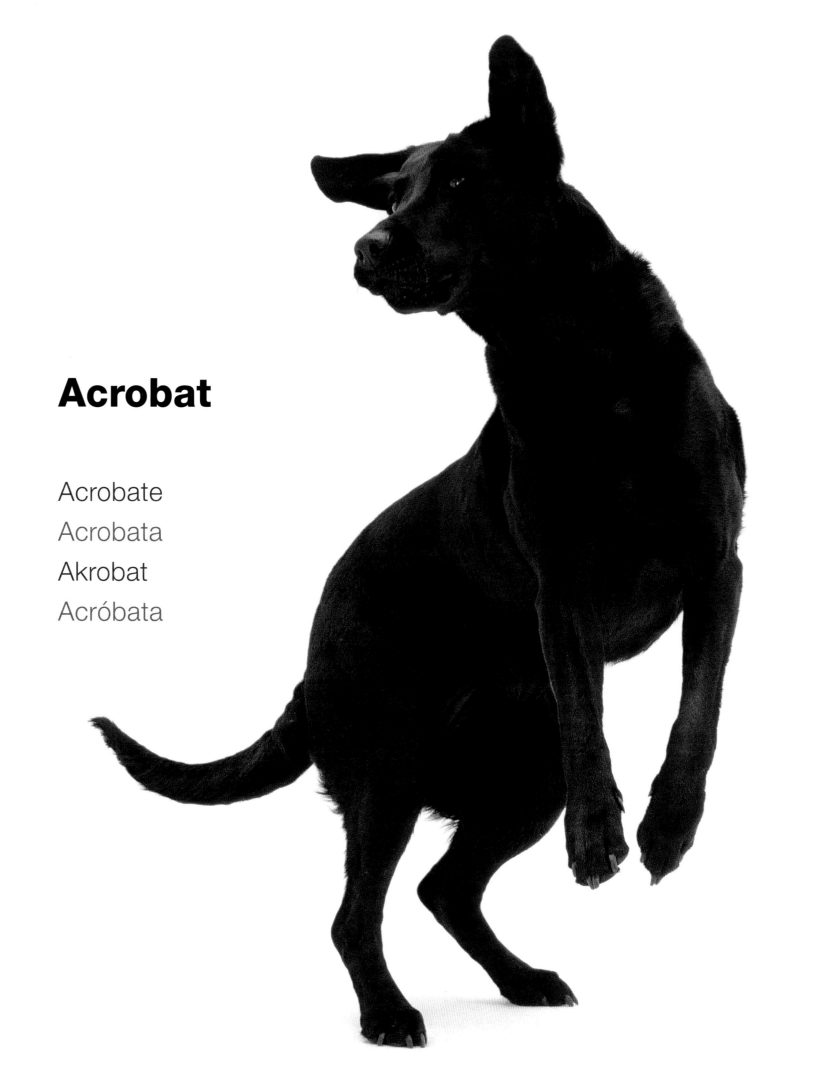

Acrobat

Acrobate
Acrobata
Akrobat
Acróbata

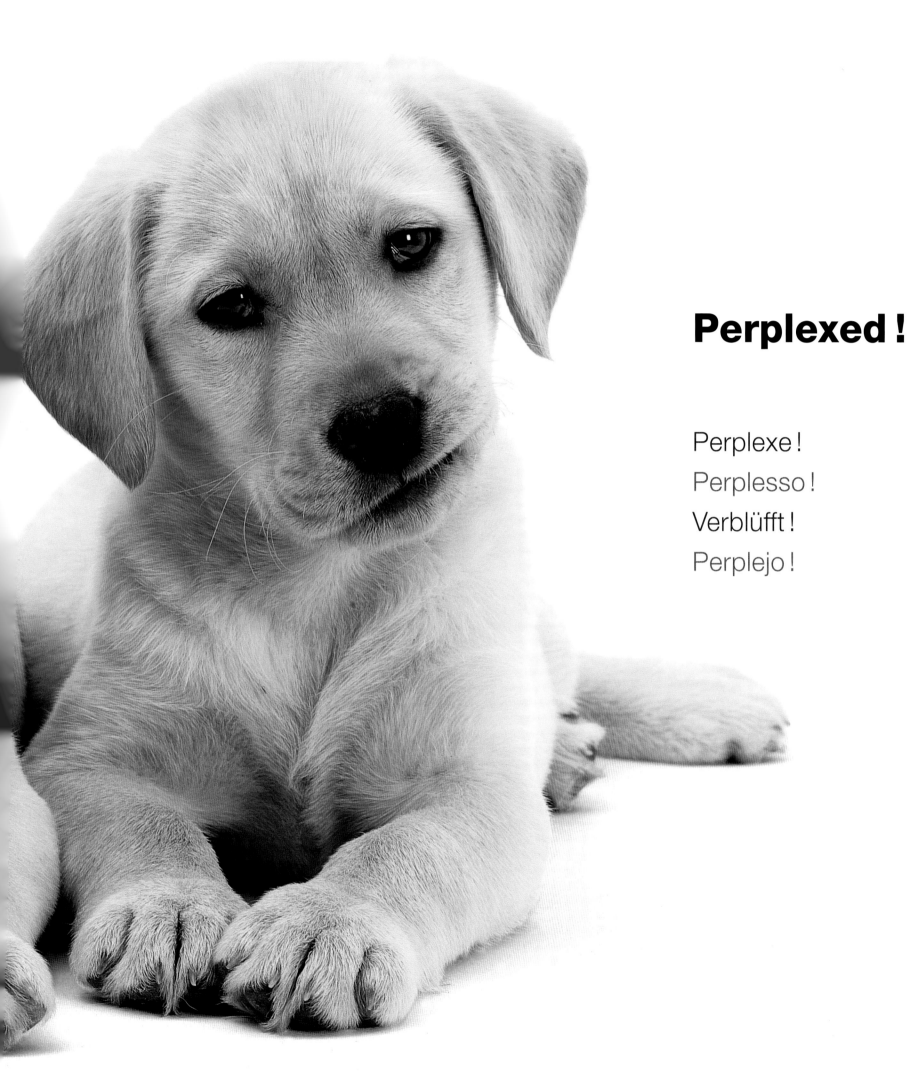

Perplexed !

Perplexe !
Perplesso !
Verblüfft !
Perplejo !

Boy sopranos

Voix d'enfants

Voci bianche

Knabenchor

Voces blancas

Cream and **Chocolate** Crème et chocolat
Panna e cioccolato
Sahne und Schokolade
Nata y chocolate

Sit !

Assis! Seduto! Sitz! Siéntate!

Gunmen

Bandits
Banditi
Banditen
Bandidos

Thoughtful

Pensif Pensieroso Nachdenklich Pensativo

Timid

Timide
Timido
Schüchtern
Tímido

Disconsolates

Inconsolables Sconsolati Untröstlich Desconsolados

Generations

Générations
Generazioni
Nachkommen
Generaciónes

1,2,3,4,5,6,7

"Photo credits"

✳ All photographs are by Araldo De Luca/Archivio White Star except the following :

✳ Sam Allen/KimballStock : pages 73, 83

✳ Jane Burton/Warren Photographic : pages 46, 49, 51, 52-53, 75, 95, 99, 101, 105, 122, 124, 125

✳ Cathy Crawford/NonStock/Getty Images : page 90

✳ John Daniels/ardea.com : pages 50, 88, 109

✳ Ron Kimball/KimballStock : page 104

✳ Lifeonwhite.com : pages 87, 94, 110, 111, 114, 115

✳ John Molloy/Getty Images : page 96 bottom

✳ Mark Taylor/Warren Photographic : pages 47, 48, 54-55, 93, 96-97, 106-107

Araldo de Luca

Araldo De Luca was born in Rome in 1952. He lived in the Italian capital and became involved in the photography of art at a very early age, and later won the prestigious Ilford Prize "Spazi ed immagini del Barocco Romano" (1980). Since 1995 his 90,000 or more renowned art pictures are catalogued in an archive which has won worldwide acclaim. Considered one of the world's greatest photographers of statuary and jewelry, De Luca has developed sophisticated lighting techniques that heighten the power of his seductive images to communicate the passion that the artists invested in their work. De Luca's great skill in the use of light, acquired while photographing wonderful statuary, enables him to work freely in other fields with amazing effects – as his portraits of dogs presented in this volume demonstrate. White Star Publishers have worked with De Luca on many volumes, including *Egyptian Treasures from the Egyptian Museum in Cairo* (1999), *Tutankhamun : the Eternal Splendor of the Boy Pharaoh* (2000), *Illustrated Guide to the Egyptian Museum in Cairo* (2003), *Valley of the Kings* (2002), *Ramesses II* (2002), *The Treasures of the Pyramids* (2003), *Pompeii* (2004), *The Eternal Army* (2005) and *A Dog's Life* (2008).

WHITE STAR PUBLISHERS

WS White Star Publishers® is a registered trademark
property of Edizioni White Star s.r.l.

© 2010 Edizioni White Star s.r.l.
Via Candido Sassone, 24
13100 Vercelli, Italy
www.whitestar.it

Editing: Elizabeth Heath

All rights reserved. No part of this publication may be reproduced,
stored in a retrieval system or transmitted in any form or by any
means, electronic, mechanical, photocopying, recording or otherwise,
without written permission from the publisher.

ISBN 978-88-544-0553-0
1 2 3 4 5 6   14 13 12 11 10

Printed in Indonesia